101 Fascinating Facts About 10 Of The Most Recognizable Companies In The World

 EntrepreneurshipFacts.com

Follow us on social media to stay updated with our new books and increase your knowledge about business and successful people on a daily basis:

Instagram   Facebook   Twitter

Also check out our website for the latest facts and articles about business and entrepreneurship:

www.EntrepreneurshipFacts.com

Introduction

I want to thank you and congratulate you for downloading the ebook "101 Fascinating Facts About 10 Of The Most Recognizable Companies In The World"

You are probably familiar with these ten companies; indeed, you are using their products and services on a daily basis.

- Walmart
- Samsung
- Apple
- Toyota
- Google
- Microsoft
- Coca-cola
- Nike
- Walt Disney
- McDonald

This book contain 101 fascinating facts that you might not know about these successful companies, from how they were founded to the current date, and what made them succeed.

It is more than just a book of knowledge allowing you to increase what you already know about widely well-known organizations, but hopefully it can inspire, motivate and benefit you in one way or another.

Table of Contents

McDonald's

McDonald's is the world's largest chain of hamburger fast food restaurants, primarily sells hamburgers, cheeseburgers, chicken products, french fries, breakfast items, soft drinks, milkshakes, and desserts. In the mid 2000s, McDonalds was forced to diversify their offering after consumer tastes began to demand healthier items. Since then, McDonald's has expanded their menu significantly to include salads, wraps, smoothies and fruit.

The company first began in 1940 as a barbeque restaurant. Operated by Richard and Maurice McDonald, they adjusted their operating strategy in 1948 to focus solely on hamburgers and implement a production line approach.

In 1955, the company secured their first franchise agent, Ray Kroc. After purchasing the chain from the McDonald brothers, he would oversee its continued growth and expand across the globe. With a main office currently located in Illinois, McDonald's has plans to move this to Chicago by 2018.

Fact #1: The company currently owns all of its property – valued at an estimated $16 to $18 billion. However, in recent times, there have been calls to spin off the company's US holdings into a potential real estate investment trust. The company earns a significant portion of its revenue from rental payments from franchisees. These rent payments have risen 26 percent over the past five years, and currently account for one fifth of the company's total revenue

Fact #2: McDonald's hires around 1 million workers in the US every year. This estimate from Fast Food Nation assumes a 700,000 domestic workforce with 150% turnover rate. According to the report, nearly one in eight workers in the U.S. have at some time been employed by McDonald's. As of 2015, McDonald's employing more than 420,000 people.

Fact #3: Believe it or not, according to QSR magazine, which serves the "quick serve" (a.k.a. fast food) restaurant industry, the world's largest toy distributor is. McDonald's! It seems that about 20% of McDonald's sales involve Happy Meals, which feature some kind of toy.

Fact #4: Back in the 1960s, McDonald's employees didn't just get the go-ahead to flip hamburgers after completing the fast food chain's employee training. Apparently, they had to receive an actual, physical diploma from the Universitas McDonald's Hambergerensis.

Today, the McDonald's training facility, Hamburger University, is still up and running. It is a 130,000-square-foot (12,000 m2) training facility of McDonald's, located in Oak Brook, Illinois, a western suburb of Chicago. This corporate university was designed to instruct personnel employed by McDonald's in the various aspects of restaurant management. More than 80,000 restaurant managers, mid-managers and owner/operators have graduated from this facility.

Fact #5: McDonald's Big Mac is used as an economic index to compare purchasing power between currencies and countries. It "seeks to make exchange-rate theory a bit more digestible."

The Big Mac index was introduced in The Economist in September 1986 by Pam Woodall as a semi-humorous illustration of purchasing power parity and has been published by that paper annually since then. The index also gave rise to the word burgernomics.

Fact #6: McDonald's' iconic golden arches are recognized by more people than the cross. A survey by Sponsorship Research International found that 88 percent could identify the arches and only 54 percent could name the Christian cross

Fact #7: Donald A. Gorske is such a fan of the burger chain that he's eaten at one of their outlets (nearly) every single day since 17 May 1972. Donald consumed his 26,000th McDonald's Big Mac on 11 October 2012, in his fortieth year of eating Big Macs on a daily basis. He also mentioned that he has had a Big Mac in every state in the US.

If you took the beef from all the Big Macs that Donald's eaten in his lifetime, you'd be faced with a single 2.3-tonne (5,200-lb) burger patty measuring a mammoth 2.6 m (8 ft 6 in) wide and 50 cm (19.6 in) thick!

Fact #8: In 1992, a woman spilled coffee on herself while sitting in the passenger seat of a car at a McDonald's drive-thru, getting third-degree burns as a result. She sued McDonald's and was awarded nearly $3 million, which was lowered to $640,000.

Documentation was released by McDonald's showing that there were more than 700 claims by people burned by coffee between 1982 and 1992.

Fact #9: The World's largest McDonald's is in Orlando. Even though the Orlando location was already the largest franchise, the store upgraded to 19,000 square feet in 2016. The store includes a bowling alley, arcade games and slides for children. The location even frequently hosts concerts and gator shows.

Fact #10: Sixty-eight million people are served every day at McDonald's, which is approximately 1 percent of the world population. McDonald's sells an average of 75 burgers a second in 119 countries across over 36,000 outlets.

Walmart

Walmart is a multi-national corporation based in the United States that owns a series of stores with a focus on value-priced or discounted retail goods. Walmart was started by a man named Sam Walton in 1962, and incorporated seven years later in 1969. By 1972, the company had been listed on the New York Stock Exchange, and between the late 80s and early 90s, had transitioned from a regional competitor to become a fierce national presence in the retail industry.

At that point in time, Walmart had historically been confined to the Southern states and lower Midwest; however, by the early 90s, the company had expanded its reach across the nation.

With its main office located in Alabama, Walmart's attempts at investing outside of North America has been met with both positive and negative outcomes. Some locations, specifically within the UK, South America and China have been highly profitable; others, such as Germany and South Korea, resulted in failure.

Fact #1: Walmart's founder, Sam Walton, was a businessman who once worked at J.C. Penney. After purchasing a branch of the Ben Franklin stores from the Butler Brothers in 1945, his main goal was to sell products for the lowest price possible and position the company as looking out for the customer's well being. This approach aims to achieve a high volume of sales, which can be profitable even with small profit margins.

After his first year, Walton saw sales rise by 45%, quickly reaching $105,000 US in revenue. Over the next four years, the store's revenue would jump by tens of thousands each year, resulting in an impressive $250,000 by its fifth year in operation.

The very first Walmart launched in Rogers, Arkansas in 1962. Over the first five years, Walmart founder Sam Walton and his brother would open an additional 23 stores and achieve over $12.7 billion in sales.

Fact #2: More than 260 million people shop at Walmart every week, and the company averages a profit of $1.8 million every hour

Despite the big profits, the company has come under fire for not passing more on to staff. A report from PayScale showed Walmart's CEO gets paid 1,034 times more than the average Walmart worker.

Fact #3: Roughly 90% of the company's international stores operate under a different name. There's Walmex in Mexico, Asda in the UK, Seiyu in Japan and Best Price in India. In total, Walmart operates under 72 different banners globally.

Fact #4: Can't get enough of Walmart? Well you're in luck as there's a Walmart museum you can roam around. The site is Sam Walton's old shop called Walton's 5&10. The museum has its original tiles and tin ceiling and is filled with toys and knick knacks from another era. There's also a '50s-style soda fountain café.

Fact #5: If you live in the U.S. you won't have to look far for a store. According to reports around 90% of Americans live within 15 minutes of a Walmart. As a result, more than 78% of Americans shop at Walmart.

Fact #6: As of July 31, 2016, Walmart's international operations comprised 6,256 stores and 800,000 workers in 26 countries outside the

United States. There are wholly owned operations in Argentina, Brazil, Canada, and the UK. With 2.2 million employees worldwide, the company is the largest private employer in the U.S. and Mexico, and one of the largest in Canada

Fact #7: It turns out you can pick up just about anything at Walmart. Psychology Today magazine published a study of "missed connection" posts on Craigslist, where love-struck hopefuls try to track down a stranger who caught their eye. The results found that Walmart is the most popular place to find love at first sight. Singles get shopping!

Here is a real story. Customer Wayne Brandenburg had been shopping at his local Walmart in North Carolina for years when he laid eyes on cashier Susan, this happened in 2005. After flirting at the check-out and visiting her several times a week, the couple finally get married in Febuary 2013. The wedding location? Walmart of course. The wedding cake was even from the store's bakery.

Fact #8: While staff are expected to have excellent customer service at all times, the company has a 10-Foot Rule implemented by Sam Walton. Here is what he said, "I want you to promise that whenever you come within 10 feet of a customer, you will look him in the eye, greet him, and ask him if you can help him."

Fact #9: Walmart's 2015 revenue was a whopping $482 billion. Those kind of profits make the company richer than many countries, including South Africa, $317.3 billion; United Arab Emirates, $339.1 billion;, Norway, $397.6 billion; Belgium, $458.7 billion; and Sweden, $483.7 billion.

Fact #10: The Waltons are the richest family in America thanks to their ironclad control over Wal-Mart. Seven heirs of founders Sam Walton and his brother James "Bud" own about half of the company's stock. According to Forbes, as of 2016 they're collectively worth $130 billion.

Samsung

A global company offering a broad array of consumer electronics and IT solutions, Samsung Electronics began in 1969 as a subsidiary of the Samsung Electronics Group. With sales networks in 80 countries and 370,000 employees, the company's main office is located in Suwon, South Korea.

Samsung Electronics' first pioneer products were mainly electronics and electrical appliances such as televisions, refrigerators, and washing machines. This, however, has seen the inclusion of a variety of other more advanced products. Samsung is a major manufacturer of electronic components such as lithium-ion batteries, semiconductors, chips, flash memory and hard drive devices for clients such as Apple, Sony, HTC and Nokia.

After a recent foray into the world of consumer electronics, Samsung has now secured its spot on the list of top mobile and smartphone manufacturers, driven predominantly by the success of the Samsung Galaxy line. In addition, Samsung has been a significant player in the tablet computer world, focusing on its Samsung Galaxy Tab collection. In fact, the company is often lauded as a leader in the phablet market due to its debut of the Samsung Galaxy Note family.

Samsung has been successful in retaining its spot as the top manufacturer of televisions in the world since 2006, and the largest manufacturer of mobile phones since 2011. Also in the year of 2011, the company replaced Apple's spot as the largest technology company worldwide, and is a significant driver of South Korea's economic success.

Fact #1: Samsung was destined for greatness from day one

Right from its founding, Lee Byung-chul believed that his new company was the start of something much bigger. The company's name choice reflected this ambition. Built from the Korean words sam (three) and sung (stars), the tri-star symbol is said to culturally represent something "big, numerous and powerful".

At it's founding, this was a pretty bold claim from a company that was nothing more than a trading company of forty employees that dealt in locally grown produce and in the creation of noodles. Since then, Samsung has certainly found its way into a lot more than just noodle-making.

Fact #2: Samsung is not just an electronics and mobile producer..

The Samsung Group has 59 unlisted companies and 19 listed, all of which have their primary listings on the Korea exchange. These companies range from constructions to financial services, ship building, and even medical.

In fact, Samsung's construction division built the Burj Khalifa, which is the tallest building in the world.

Fact #3: The first electronics product produced by Samsung was a black and white TV in 1970. The company expanded a great deal in the decades to follow, and in 1986 entered into the mobile game with a car phone. While Samsung's early TV efforts were fairly well received, the first car phone from the company was poorly received and had terrible sales as a result.

Fact #4: Although Samsung had been a significant player in the electronics and mobile industry for a number of decades, Samsung Chairman Lee Kun-hee (above) truly changed the game for the company in 1993. Armed with a new management philosophy, he believed strongly in the importance of focusing on product quality.

Claiming to have a focus on quality and fully committing to it can be vastly different, and Samsung quickly realized this. It was 1995; two years after Lee had communicated the company's decision to focus on quality. After reportedly becoming frustrated with the still poor quality

Samsung's products, Lee wanted to make a statement. To communicate his dedication to quality, he asked for phones, televisions, fax machines and a variety of other equipment to be stacked in a pile, only to be destroyed with heavy hammers.

While this type of demonstration may seem extreme, it served to drive home his point to the close to 2000 employees at the time. While over $50 million worth of the company's inventory was destroyed, a new pathway for Samsung had emerged. Dramatic enough to instigate a change, this show would serve to usher in a new period of quality and increased growth across the globe. Over the coming decades, Samsung would see continued success due to this pivotal change to the company's core values.

Fact #5: The Samsung SCH-100 was released back in 1996, making it the very first phone to utilize CDMA technology. Back in the day, CDMA was fairly a new technology and this was before the era of 4G internet connections, therefore CDMA was well received.

Fact #6: Yes, the Gear family has had variants that have allowed you to text or even make calls without needing to tether your phone, but the watch phone market actually begins much earlier – back in 1999. Samsung was the first pioneer, and one of the only ones since, to build a watch that also doubled as a phone. This bad boy was dubbed the Samsung SPH-WP10.

This unique watch phone could not only tell time, it also could make phone calls for up to 90 minutes. After that, the battery would be depleted and you'd have to run over to a charger.

The screen was of the back-lit monochrome LCD variety, and there were physical buttons navigating around the menu. There were even voice commands for dialing your contacts – fancy.

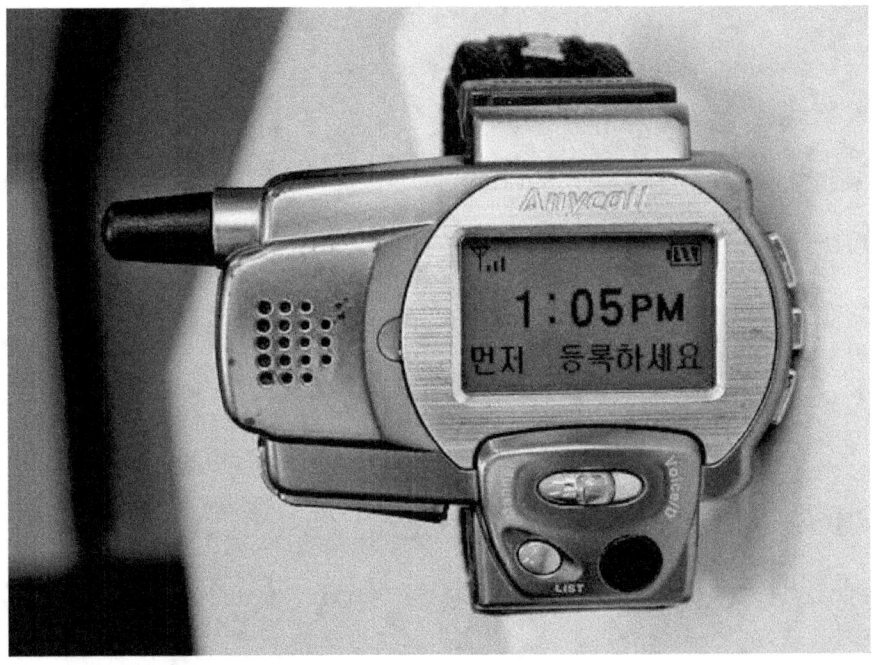

Fact #7: Samsung may not be the first to make a smartphone by any means, but they were one of the first players to truly get aggressive about the market and introduced the first "PDA phone" with a color display in the US market in 2001.

Called the SPH-i300, this phone was designed for Sprint's network and ran on Palm OS and had all the functions of a normal PDA, with the added bonus of making calls.

Fact #8: The key to a winning product? Quality, right? Well, that certainly helps but in reality, marketing is often just as – if not more – important. You can have the greatest product ever, but if no one ever learns about it, it really won't matter. In order to keep Samsung on the public's radar, Samsung spends a ton of dough, much more than anyone else out there.

How much we talking about? In 2013, it was around $4 billion for advertising, and the costs have likely gotten higher, not lower. That's in addition to another $5 billion spent in 'general marketing'.

Fact # 9: On October 19, 2011, Samsung was fined EUR 145,727,000 for being part of a price cartel of ten companies for selling DRAMs, which lasted from 1 July 1998 to 15 June 2002. DRAM is widely used in digital electronics where low-cost and high-capacity memory is required.

The company received, like most of the other members of the cartel, a 10-% reduction for acknowledging the facts to investigators. Samsung had to pay 90% of their share of the settlement, but Micron (one of the ten companies involved) avoided payment as a result of having initially revealed the case to investigators.

Fact # 10: Samsung has a powerful influence on South Korea's economic development, politics, media and culture. Its affiliate companies produce around a fifth of South Korea's total exports. Samsung's revenue was equal to 17% of South Korea's $1,082 billion GDP.

Google

Google is a technology company focused on providing Internet-related services and products. With a mission to "organize the world's information to make it universally accessible and useful," Google has been very successful from its venture into AdWords, a digital advertising service that positions ads pertaining to a user's search above the regular search results.

Google's consistent growth has resulted in a number of new products being development, acquisitions and a variety of partnerships, expanding their offering significantly. Over the past 15 years, consumers have seen the launch of Gmail and Google Drive, the development of an Android mobile operating system, and creation of the Chrome OS, which operates using only Chrome browser.

Fact #1: Google began in January 1996 as a research project by Larry Page and Sergey Brin when they were both PhD students at Stanford University in Stanford, California.

While conventional search engines ranked results by counting how many times the search terms appeared on the page, the two theorized about a better system that analyzed the relationships between websites. They called this new technology PageRank; it determined a website's relevance by the number of pages, and the importance of those pages, that linked back to the original site.

Fact #2: The company's search engine algorithm was stored on 10 separate 4GB hard drives. What's odd about it is that Sergey Brin and Larry Page decided to construct their hard drive storage tower out of Lego. This allowed the two to expand the storage capacity easily, rather than having to find and pay for more expensive structures as their project grew. Today Google has indexed more than 100 million gigabytes of data, making its original 40 GB storage capacity look rather humble.

Fact #3: When Larry Page was granted a patent for the Google's search algorithm it was assigned to Stanford. Therefore when the two left to form

Google, Stanford received 1.8 million shares of Google stock in exchange for a long-term patent license.

PageRank has since earned more than $337 million for Stanford, which was more than enough to see the two inducted into the university's Inventor Hall of Frame.

Fact #4: Google was originally named "BackRub", because the system checked backlinks to estimate the importance of a site. Eventually, they changed the name to Google, originating from a misspelling of the word "googol", the number one followed by one hundred zeros, which was picked to signify that the search engine was intended to provide large quantities of information.

Fact #5: Google has a fair bit of land over at Mountain View, which obviously needs to be trimmed and kept free of weeds to keep up appearances. Instead of breaking out the mowers and strimmers, Google pays for some goats to do the job.

The company hires out a heard of 200 goats from California Grazing to trim the lawns. The animals spend a week chewing on the grass and fertilizing the land. Apparently this costs the same as it would to bring in the lawn mowers, and Google says that goats are a lot more environmentally friendly and cuter to watch, too.

Fact #6: Google has a very cool and secret way of recruiting engineers
If you do a search on Google for something sufficiently tech-y, Google's search results page will offer users a challenge wherein they can see

if their technical skills are up to snuff with what Google is looking for. From there, users who successfully pass a number of subsequent technical and coding challenges can land an interview at the search giant.

Word of Google's clever recruiting campaign was initially made public via an August 2015 blogpost from Max Rosett. Rosetta eventually got a job at Google. He says of his experience: It's a "brilliant recruiting tactic. Google used it to identify me before I had even applied anywhere else, and they made me feel important while doing so. At the same time, they respected my privacy and didn't reach out to me without explicitly requesting my information."

Fact #7: When a Google employee dies, their spouses receive half pay from the company for 10 years and their children US$1,000 per month until they turn 19.

Fact #8: If you type in "I want to commit suicide" into Google's search bar, the top result will be for the National Suicide Prevention lifeline with an accompanying phone number and a link to chat with a trained professional.

Fact #9: The word "Google" was added to the dictionary in 2006 as a verb. It is officially listed as a transitive verb: "to use the Google search engine to obtain information about (as a person) on the World Wide Web."

Fact #10: When Google started its initial public offering, Larry Page wanted the buyers to take a test prior to buying Google stock. His philosophy behind this was that the buyers should be well aware of what Google is all about. However, the US Securities and Exchange Commission did not allow it.

The company went public on August 19, 2004 with a starting price of just only $85 per share for about 19.6 million shares at the time. Today the company's stock price has gone up over 1,500%.

Coca-cola

The Coca-Cola Company produces a carbonated soft drink and is headquartered in Atlanta, Georgia. John Pemberton, an American pharmacist, created Coca-Cola in the late 19th century, with initial plans to use it as a patent medicine. However, the company was later purchased by Asa Griggs Candler. Candler was a businessman whose successful implementation of marketing strategies would establish Coke's position as a fierce competitor in the soft drink industry.

Since 1889, Coca-Cola's has continued to operate using a franchised approach. Even in the early days when the company only produced syrup concentrate, it would be sold to a variety of bottling companies throughout the world who retained the rights to distribute throughout certain areas. As of 2013, Coke products are present in more than 200 countries, with consumers downing more than 1.8 billion company beverage servings each day

Fact #1: Coca-Cola was originally created by John Pemberton as a substitute for his morphine addiction. It was an alcoholic drink at first and the alcohol was later removed during the prohibition period.

John Pemberton, was wounded during the American Civil War. To find relief from the pain he got addicted to morphine but felt a need to stop it. Finding inspiration from a French coca wine, he developed a prototype in Pemberton's Eagle Drug and Chemical House. The drink was first sold in Atlanta as a patent medicine for five cents per glass. It was a time when people in United States thought soda water was good for health and Pemberton sold his drink claiming it cured many neurological diseases and even impotence

Fact #2: The very first Coca-Cola products contained cocaine — around 9 milligrams per glass. Cocaine was removed from Coca-Cola in 1903.

Fact #3: If every drop of Coke ever produced were placed in 8-ounce bottles and laid end-to-end, the bottles would reach the moon and back more than 2,000 times.

Fact #4: Coca-Cola believes it invented the concept of the coupon. The company distributed sample coupons in late 1886, and the company believes it was the reason the drink spread from the small population of Atlanta to every state in the US by 1990. Between 1886 and 1914, one in 10 Cokes was given away free.

Fact #5: Coca-Cola is also to thank for the image we have today of Santa Claus. Coke began its Christmas advertising in 1920s to drum up sales in the slow winter months. It used several images, but none proved popular until 1931 when illustrator Haddon Sundblom painted a plump, jolly Santa in a red coat. The image was based on the Clement Moore poem "A Visit from St. Nicholas" and his own Scandinavian heritage. Previous images of Santa Claus ranged from him being gaunt, to very big, and he wore all different colors including green and brown.

Fact #6: The company has operated a franchised distribution system since 1889, wherein The Coca-Cola Company only produces syrup concentrate, which is then sold to various bottlers throughout the world who hold exclusive territories. The bottlers then produce the finished product in cans and bottles from the concentrate, in combination with filtered water and sweeteners

Fact #7: Only 2 people alive know the "recipe" of Coca-Cola. It's such protected secret that they are both not allowed to travel on the same plane at the same time in case it crashes.

Coca-cola has never patented the formula, saying to do so would require its disclosure. And once the patent expired, anyone would be able to use that recipe to produce a generic version of the world famous drink.

Since its creation in 1886, the recipe was only passed through word of mouth until a group of investors write it down in 1919. For over 86 years the formula was locked in the bank of Atlanta later to be moved into their own secure private vault. The company has built a multi-million vault in their headquarters in Atlanta specifically to guard the secret formula for the soft-drink.

Fact #8: As of 2016, Coca-Cola ranked #5 on the Forbes list of the World's Most Valuable Brands with a brand value of $58.5 billion. In fact, the red and white Coca-Cola logo is recognized by 94% of the world's population. Coca-Cola has also reported that it's name is the second-most understood term in the world, behind "okay."

Fact #9: 3.1% of all beverages consumed around the world are Coca-Cola products. Of the 55 billion servings of all kinds of beverages drunk each day (other than water), 1.7 billion are Coca-Cola trademarked/licensed drinks.

Fact #10: Coca-Cola makes so many different types of beverages that it would take you over 9 years to taste them all if you tried one per day. According to Coca-Cola India, the company has over 500 active brands with 3, 500 different types of products including 800 low calorie alternatives. Coca-Cola has a long history of brand acquisitions including famous brands such as Minute Maid, Thums Up, Fanta, Sprite and Bacardi.

Microsoft

Microsoft Corporation is a technology company whose primary focus is developing, manufacturing and selling software, computer electronics and computers. In addition to creating and selling their products, Microsoft has achieved significant success from licensing and support of these products. With a head office in Redmond, Washington, Microsoft is widely renowned for its Windows line of operating systems, Microsoft Office Suite, and its browser, Internet Explorer. However, Microsoft's foray into hardware development included the Xbox video game console and the Microsoft Surface tablet. In 2011, Microsoft's revenue secured it a spot as the world's largest software developer, and consequently one of the most valuable companies in the world.

Fact #1: If you bought one share of Microsoft stock for $21 at its March 13, 1986, IPO, it would be worth $14,990 today. That's a whopping 71,283% increase over 30 years.

The company's 1986 initial public offering (IPO), and subsequent rise in its share price, created three billionaires and an estimated 12,000 millionaires among Microsoft employees.

Fact #2: In 1987, at age 31, Microsoft cofounder Bill Gates became the youngest billionaire ever at the time. In 1995, he'd become the world's richest man with a net worth of $12.9 billion. Since then, Bill Gates frequently topping the list of the world's richest man.

Fact #3: Microsoft and Apple actually worked together for years on software for the first

Macintosh computer — until Microsoft announced its competing Windows, which sparked a rivalry between Bill Gates and Steve Jobs that lasted for decades. However, in 1997, Microsoft saved Apple from almost certain bankruptcy by making a $150 million investment. Steve Jobs announced it on stage at his first appearance as Apple CEO, to boos from the audience.

Fact #4: Microsoft loves to celebrate events with M&M candies, in fact, its kind of a tradition in the company since a long time. If you are an employee celebrating your birthday, you need to give 1 pound of M&Ms for every year you've worked at Microsoft.

Fact #5: Microsoft introduced their first Windows XP-based tablet in 2001, but only contributed to the biggest blunders in their history. It was a touchscreen tablet with a stylus and a keyboard.

Fact #6: Microsoft once sued a high school student named Mike Rowe who registered the domain MikeRoweSoft.com for his part-time web-design business. A settlement was finally reached that included sending the teenager an X-Box in exchange for the domain.

Fact #7: Microsoft spent hundreds of millions of dollars advertising Windows 95

It wasn't until Windows 95 was released in August 1995 that Microsoft truly became a dominant force in desktop computing. With an advertising budget that some peg as high as $300 million, Microsoft's Windows 95 launch event was an exercise in excess. The launch itself featured Jay Leno cracking wise, a Rolling Stones theme song, and all sorts of other extravagant gestures. Though perhaps a bit over the top, the payoff was immense. Over the next 10 years or so, Microsoft's annual revenue climbed by more than five times.

Fact #8: The Microsoft Surface team worked in secret behind the company's Studio B building in Redmond. Many Microsoft's employees didn't even know what was going on behind doors under security guard. It's rumored that the door leads to an underground bunker.

Fact #9: Microsoft doesn't sell software. The firm licenses its software, retaining full ownership rights. Buyers of the software must pay Microsoft for the right to use it, a system developed by Bill Gates in 1976.

Fact #10: Microsoft passed on the opportunity to acquire YouTube for $500 million back in 2006. Six months later Google paid $1.65 billion for the site that is now the most popular video destination on the Web.

Toyota

With a head office in Toyota, Aichi, Japan, Toyota Motor Corporation is an automotive manufacturer and one of the world's largest companies. With over 330,000 employees, the company ranks 13 across the globe in terms of revenue. In 2012, Toyota secured their place as the largest auto manufacturer in the world, and the company declared they had produced a total of 200 million vehicles.

Founded by Kiichiro Toyoda, the company origin started in 1934 as a department of Toyota Industries, his father's company. The company's first product was the Type A engine; and in 1936, Toyota produced its first passenger car, the Toyota AA. Kiichiro Toyoda officially registered his company in August 1937 as the Toyota Motor Company.

Fact #1: Toyota was originally named Toyoda, from the family name of the company's founder, Kiichirō Toyoda. But Risaburō Toyoda, who had married into the family and was not born with that name, preferred "Toyota" because it took eight brush strokes (a lucky number) to write in Japanese, was visually simpler (leaving off the diacritic at the end), and with a voiceless consonant instead of a voiced one (voiced consonants are considered to have a "murky" or "muddy" sound compared to voiceless consonants, which are "clear"). Since toyoda literally means "fertile rice paddies", changing the name also prevented the company from being associated with old-fashioned farming.

Fact #2: From September 1947, Toyota's small-sized vehicles were sold under the name "Toyopet". The company entered the American market in 1957 with the Toyopet Crown, the name was not well received due to connotations of toys and pets. However, the US is one of Toyota's largest markets today.

Fact #3: Toyota operates under relatively few brand names, unlike some other auto manufacturers. The only other wholly-owned brands under Toyota are luxury brand Lexus and entry-level brand Scion.

Other than Lexus and Scion, Toyota owns a controlling stake in Hino, a commercial truck and bus manufacturer, and Daihatsu, a manufacturer of small city cars. Toyota also owns a minority stake in Subaru's parent company.

Fact #4: Despite a longstanding reputation for reliability, Toyota set a record in 2009 for the number of vehicles recalled (most for unintended acceleration issues).

Fact #5: Toyota is the world's market leader in sales of hybrid electric vehicles, and one of the largest companies to encourage the mass-market adoption of hybrid vehicles across the globe. Cumulative global sales of Toyota and Lexus hybrid passenger car models passed the 9 million milestone in April 2016. Its Prius family is the world's top selling hybrid nameplate with almost 5.7 million units sold worldwide as of 30 April 2016

Fact #6: According to the statistics, Corolla is the bestselling nameplate for vehicles all over the world. As of 2013, the total number of Toyota Corolla nameplates that have been sold is 30 million, which is astonishing. What is even more astonishing is that it has been the best-selling nameplate since 1997 when the cumulative sales went over 30 million units. You would think that it would have a stronger competition in today's automobile market but Corolla still stands out as the best-selling one.

Fact #7: Toyota was about to go bankrupt in the 1950s, producing only 300 trucks in 1950. Then came the Korean War and the United States ordered 5000 vehicles for the war effort, which revived the company. The Korean War is also where the Land Cruiser (pictured) made its debut.

Fact #8: Toyota has been in the business of manufacturing prefabricated homes since 1975 and has sold around 250,000 homes and counting since then. The houses are built with environmentally friendly materials and, since this is Japan we're talking about, are earthquake-proof. Prices range from $200k-800k.

Fact #9: People say that Toyotas run forever, and that is not far from the truth. Statistics show that eighty percent of Toyotas that were sold 20 years ago are still on the road today.

Fact #10: Toyota has been working on fuel cell technology for over 20 years with the creation of the first fuel cell stack. At the 2014 Los Angeles Auto Show, Toyota became the first to introduce a hydrogen fuel-cell vehicle. Fuel cell vehicles use hydrogen gas to power an electric motor. Unlike conventional vehicles, which run on gasoline or diesel, fuel cell cars and trucks combine hydrogen and oxygen to produce electricity.

Walt Disney

The Walt Disney Company is a media and entertainment company with a head office in Burbank, California. As the second largest media company in the world, based on revenue, the company was historically renowned for its film studio.

The company is comprised of Walt Disney Parks and Resorts, Disney Media Networks, and Disney Consumer Products and Interactive media. However, Walt Disney Studios is one of the most recognized and high-caliber studios in the film industry.

Mickey Mouse, a highly recognized cartoon character created by the company in its early days, has served as Disney's main symbol and mascot for decades.

Fact #1: Disney was founded on October 16, 1923, by Walt Disney and Roy O. Disney as the Disney Brothers Cartoon Studio, and established itself as a leader in the American animation industry

Fact #2: Mickey Mouse was originally named Mortimer because Disney's wife, Lillian, disliked the sound of 'Mortimer Mouse'. Mickey mouse quickly became a success in 1928, and Walt Disney also provided the voice for his creation in the early years.

Fact #3: Disney took a massive risk producing the world's first feature-length animated movie in 1937's Snow White and the Seven Dwarfs, which required a then-enormous $1.499 million production budget. Industry skeptics called the project "Disney's Folly" before it even hit theaters.

Snow White turned out to be a huge commercial success, grossing over $66 million during its 1937 theatrical run before reaching $185 million with the help of rereleases in 1983, 1987, and 1993. Today, Snow White's inflation-adjusted box office total of $885 million ranks it as the 10th highest-grossing domestic movie of all time.

Fact #4: After completing Disneyland in 1955, Disney almost opened a ski resort. The site would have been near California's Sequoia National Park, was meant to accommodate as many as 20,000 skiers, and progressed so far that Disney even acquired Forest Service approval and a roads deal with the Governor of California. After Walt Disney's death in 1966, however, the company chose to instead focus on completing its ambitious Walt Disney World project, which opened in 1971.

Fact #5: While most investors associate the Disney brand with its legendary feature films and amusement parks, the company's largest revenue generating segment is its media networks business. This segment, which accounts for more than 43% of total revenue, includes Disney's broadcast and cable television networks, TV production operations, TV distribution, domestic TV stations and radio networks.

Disney's cable networks include ESPN, Disney Channels Worldwide, ABC Family and SOAPnet. In addition, Disney also owns 50% of the A&E

Television Network, which operates A&E, History, Bio, H2, Lifetime, and LMN.

Fact #6: The company's Walt Disney World Resort, located in Orlando, Florida, employs more than 62,000 people, making it the largest single-site employer in the country. Disney World, which includes the Magic Kingdom, Epcot, Hollywood Studios, and the Animal Kingdom, spans approximately 25,000 acres (about the size of San Francisco).

Fact #7: During WWII, the U.S. and Canadian governments commissioned Disney to produce several training and propaganda films. By 1942, roughly 90% of the company's employees were actively working on war-related films, such as "Victory Through Air Power" and "Education for Death." In addition, Disney produced several anti-Hitler shorts meant to boost U.S. morale at home, including Academy Award-winning "Der Fuehrer's Face," which featured Donald Duck.

Fact #8: Since 1991, Disney's total annual revenue has only decreased twice – once in 2002 and again in 2009. In 2002, revenues dipped slightly after the company slashed operating, labor, annual live-action film, and internet costs in the prior year.

In 2009, revenues fell 4% – the company cited the global economic downturn and an acceleration of secular challenges as the main reasons behind the dip. A closer look at the books shows that only Disney's Parks and Resorts, Studio Entertainment, and Interactive Media segments logged in lower revenues than a year prior.

Fact #9: Believe it or not, Steve Jobs had an alliance with the Walt Disney Company and the acquisition of Pixar Studios. In 1986, Jobs acquired the computer graphics division of Lucasfilm Ltd. and renamed it Pixar Animation Studios. On May 5, 2006, Pixar was acquired by The Walt Disney Company, at which time Steve Jobs became Disney's largest individual shareholder at 7% and a member of Disney's Board of Directors.

Fact #10: Some of Disney's animated family films have drawn fire for being accused of having sexual references hidden in them, among them The Little Mermaid (1989), Aladdin (1992), and The Lion King (1994). Instances of sexual material hidden in some versions of The Rescuers (1977) and Who Framed Roger Rabbit (1988) resulted in recalls and modifications of the films to remove such content.

Nike

Nike, Inc. is a worldwide corporation that develops, manufactures and sells footwear, apparel, equipment, accessories and services pertaining to athletics. With a main office in Beaverton, Oregon, Nike has retained its spot as one of the largest suppliers of athletic shoes and apparel in the world, and a key player in sports equipment manufacturing.

Promoting products under the Nike brand, the company has also established other brands including Nike Golf, Nike Pro, Air Jordan and a variety of others. Nike's reach also extends to various subsidiaries such as Brand Jordan, Hurley International and Converse.

Beyond their manufacturing focus, the company also manages a number of retail establishments under the Niketown brand. In addition, under the tagline "just do it," Nike's sponsorship of high-profile athletes and sports teams has created additional recognition on a global scale.

Fact #1: The company was founded on January 25, 1964, as Blue Ribbon Sports, by Bill Bowerman and Phil Knight. It was nearly renamed Dimension Six before the name Nike was selected. The name Nike comes from the Greek goddess of victory, and It's pronounced "ny'kee".

The company initially operated as a distributor for Japanese shoe maker Onitsuka Tiger (now ASICS), making most sales at track meets out of Knight's automobile.

Fact #2: The Nike swoosh was designed by Carolyn Davidson, a Portland State University student, for just $35. She was later given stock now worth more than $640,000.

The logo conveys motion and speed in its design; it also symbolizes the wing of Nike, the Greek Goddess of Victory. When first released, the design was displayed in a variety of colors in order to stand out on the track from other shoe manufacturers. Nike then traditionally used the red and white color palette on its logo for much of its history. The red is meant to exemplify passion, energy and joy, while the white color represents nobility, charm and purity.

Fact #3: According to Ad agency Moosylvania, Nike is millennials' favorite brand, holding 62% of the athletic-shoe market. Data shows that this generation believes exercise is essential for health; this leads to increased athletic apparel and footwear spending.

Fact #4: Nike's first pair of running shoes was inspired by waffles. Nike co-founder Bill Bowerman, who was a track and field coach at the time, had been searching for a way to make shoes lighter and faster. He was having breakfast with his wife one morning in 1971 when it dawned on him that the grooves in the waffle iron she was using would be an excellent mold for a running shoe. So he grabbed his wife's waffle iron and began experimenting. He managed to succeed in his experiments, but I imagine his breakfast waffles carried a strange aftertaste thereafter.

Fact #5: In March 1987, Nike began using the 1968 Beatles track 'Revolution' in a well-known TV ad campaign. Despite licensing the song from Michael Jackson and EMI for a mere $250,000, this didn't sit well with the surviving Beatles, who felt that songwriter John Lennon would have rightly had a conniption over his revolutionary song being used to sell sneakers. In July 1987, Apple

Corps took Nike, ad agency Weiden+Kennedy, Jackson and EMI to court, successfully getting a fat financial settlement and the ad campaign pulled off the air by March 1988.

Fact #6: Footwear Brand Cole Haan Was Originally A Nike Brand. Designer footwear brand Cole Haan was originally a part of the Nike worldwide conglomerate. However, by 2012, Nike decided that the brand was too much of a financial drain on the parent company, so they sold it to Apax Partners Worldwide for a reported $570 million.

Fact #7: In 1982, Nike aired its first national television ads, created by newly formed ad agency Wieden+Kennedy (W+K), during the broadcast of the New York Marathon. The Cannes Advertising Festival has named Nike its

Advertiser of the Year in 1994 and 2003, making it the first company to receive that honor twice.

Nike also has earned the Emmy Award for best commercial twice since the award was first created in the 1990s. The first was for "The Morning After," a satirical look at what a runner might face on the morning of January 1, 2000 if every dire prediction about the Y2K problem came to fruition. The second was for a 2002 spot called "Move," which featured a series of famous and everyday athletes in a variety of athletic pursuits.

Fact #8: During the 1990s, Nike faced criticism for the use of child labor in Cambodia and Pakistan in factories it contracted to manufacture soccer balls. Although Nike took action to curb or at least reduce the practice, they continue to contract their production to companies that operate in areas where inadequate regulation and monitoring make it hard to ensure that child labor is not being used.

In 2001, a BBC documentary uncovered occurrences of child labor and poor working conditions in a Cambodian factory used by Nike. The documentary focused on six girls, who all worked seven days a week, often 16 hours a day.

Fact #9: Nike has contracted with more than 700 shops around the world and has offices located in 45 countries outside the United States. Most of the factories are located in Asia.

Fact #10: Nike has been criticized for contracting with factories (known as Nike sweatshops) in countries such as China, Vietnam, Indonesia and Mexico. Vietnam Labor Watch, an activist group, has documented that factories contracted by Nike have violated minimum wage and overtime laws in Vietnam as late as 1996, although Nike claims that this practice has been stopped.

The company has been subject to much critical coverage of the often poor working conditions and exploitation of cheap overseas labor employed in the free trade zones where their goods are typically manufactured. Sources for this criticism include Naomi Klein's book No Logo and Michael Moore documentaries.

Apple

Apple is an American company with a main office located in Cupertino, California. With a focus on designing, developing and selling consumer electronics, computer software and online services, Apple has produced a number of products that have been met with great success. The company's hardware includes a range of products including the iPhone, iPad, Macbook, iPod, Apple Watch, and even Apple TV. Apple has also delved into the software world, developing operating systems such as OS X and iOS, the media player iTunes, a web browser and various productivity apps. The past decade has seen continued expansion Apple's offering, with the company launching a variety of online services such as iTunes, the App Stores, and the renowned online storage service, iCloud.

Fact #1: Apple was founded on April 1st of 1976 to develop and sell personal computers. It was incorporated as Apple Computer, Inc. in January 1977, and was renamed as Apple Inc. in January 2007 to reflect its shifted focus toward consumer electronics.

It wasn't until 2011's posthumous biography "Steve Jobs" that we found out where Apple got its name: Turns out, Steve Jobs had been on a "fruitarian" kick and just really liked apples.

Fact #2: Besides Steve Jobs and Steve Wozniak, Apple had a third cofounder, Ronald Wayne. Serving as the venture's "adult supervision", Wayne drew the first Apple logo, wrote the three men's original partnership agreement, and wrote the Apple I manual.

He received a 10% stake in Apple but relinquished his equity for US$800 less than two weeks later, on April 12, 1976. As of April 2016, Wayne's 10% stake in Apple would be worth almost $60 billion.

Fact #3: In the '80s and '90s, facing continually shrinking Mac sales, Apple tried making everything from digital cameras, to video game consoles, and even clothing lines.

Fact #4: When Steve Jobs came back to Apple as CEO in 1997, the company was in such bad shape that his first Macworld keynote included the news that Microsoft was investing $150 million in the company — delivered by a gigantic video of Bill Gates towering over the assembly. "We need all the help we can get," Jobs said, to boos from the audience.

In fact, by 1997, Apple's financial situation was so dire that Dell CEO and founder Michael Dell, one of Microsoft's biggest partners, once said that if he were in Jobs' shoes, he'd "shut it down and give the money back to the shareholders."

Fact #5: The "i" in 1998's "iMac" is for "Internet," since it originally took only two steps to connect to the web, in case you were wondering. But Apple has also said that it stands for "individuality" and "innovation." The naming scheme continues on through the iPhone and iPad.

Fact #6: In 2011, Apple made waves when it came out that it had more cash in the bank than the US Treasury.

According to the daily statement from the U.S. Treasury, in the month of July 2011, the government had an operating cash balance of $73.8 billion. On the other hand, Apple's earnings report showed that the company had $76.2 billion in cash and marketable securities at the end of June that year.

Fact #7: Before Steve Jobs death in 2011, he presented his proposal for a new Apple campus to the Cupertino City Council. His goal was to create the best office building in the world.

The new Apple Campus will be set in a 2.8 million-square-foot area; that's a 176-acre site. It will house more than 13,000 Apple employees in one building. The building is more than a mile around. There will be 300,000 square feet of research facilities and underground parking. And the best part is that it will look like a giant alien spaceship! The construction on the campus started in 2013 with a completion date set for late 2016.

Fact #8: Fortune magazine named Apple the most admired company in the United States in 2008, and in the world from 2008 to 2012. On September 30, 2013, Apple surpassed Coca-Cola to become the world's most valuable brand in the Omnicom Group's "Best Global Brands" report.

Boston Consulting Group has ranked Apple as the world's most innovative brand every year since 2005.

As of 2016, Apple ranked number 1 on Forbes' list of the World's Most Valuable Brands with an estimated brand value of $154.1 billion. That is nearly twice as much as Google, who comes second at $82.5 billion.

Fact #9: It's Harder To Get A Job At The Apple Store Than It Is To Get Into Harvard

At a press event in 2009, Apple said that 10,000 people submitted applications to work at the new store on Manhattan's Upper West Side. Of those, just over 200 got jobs, for a 2% acceptance rate. Meanwhile, Harvard's acceptance rate was 7% in that same year, according to a March report in the

Boston Globe. That's 29,000 applications for about 2,000 admissions.

Fact #10: If you use iTunes, you have already agreed not to use Apple products to create nuclear weapons.

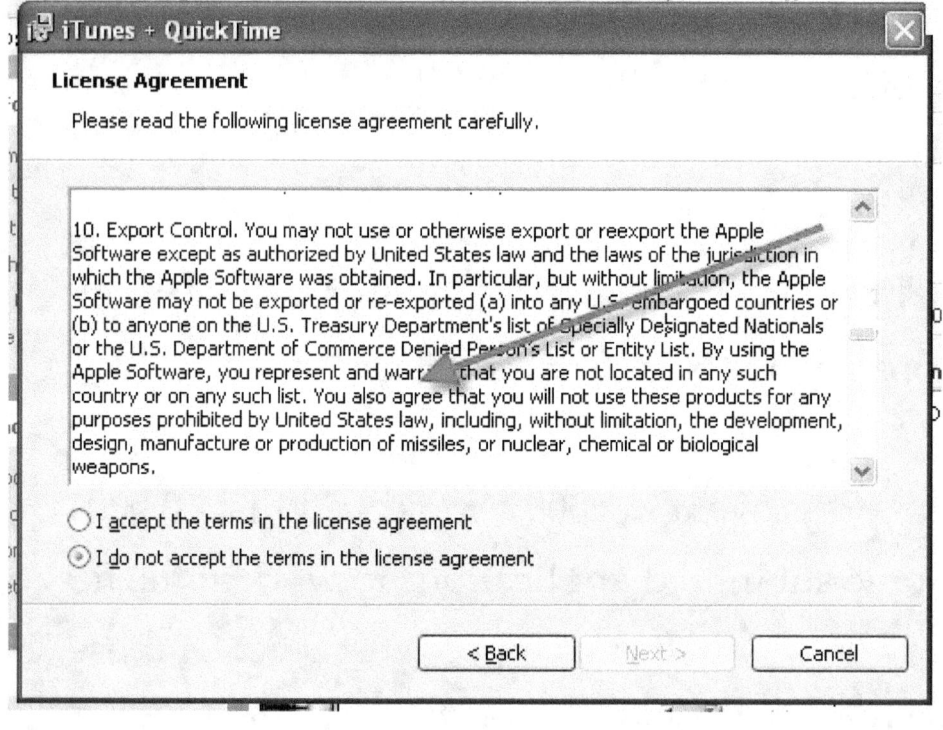

Fact #11: A rare Apple-1 computer built in Steve Jobs' garage in the summer of 1976 sold at an auction for a record-breaking $905,000. There are, at most, just 15 fully functional Apple-1 computers in existence. The high price tag — almost double the original estimated value — makes this particular Apple-1 model the world's most valuable computer relic and the most expensive Apple computer ever sold.

Conclusion

Thank you for purchasing this book and reading it this far. I hope you have learned something valuable from these most recognizable companies in the world.

Finally, if you enjoyed this book, then I'd like to ask you for a favor, would you be kind enough to leave a review for this book on Amazon? Tell us what you like or dislike and what we can improve. Your feedbacks will be greatly appreciated!

https://www.amazon.com/dp/B01LXN2JGG

Also follow EntrepreneurshipFacts on social media to stay updated with our new books and increase your knowledge about business and successful people on a daily basis:

<u>Instagram</u>   <u>Facebook</u>   <u>Twitter</u>

Check out our website for the latest facts and
articles about business and entrepreneurship:

<u>www.EntrepreneurshipFacts.com</u>

More books by Entrepreneurship Facts

101 Entrepreneurial Facts About 10 of The Most
Successful BILLIONAIRES That Can Inspire You:
What you can learn from their successes

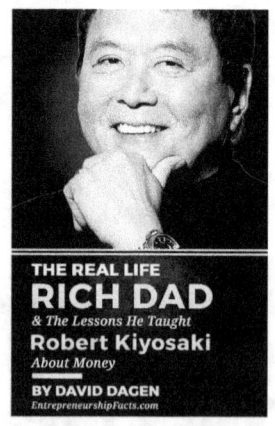

The Real Life RICH DAD & The Lessons He
Taught ROBERT KIYOSAKI about Money

Warren Buffett - 41 Fascinating Facts about Life &

Investing Philosophy: The Lessons From A

Legendary Investor

Elon Musk - Top 10 Business Lessons Through

An Inspiring Life Of A Visionary Entrepreneur:

DONALD TRUMP - Top 5 Business Lessons

From The Presidential Campaign Of A

Businessman: The Art Of Getting Attention

Richard Branson - Top 13 Secrets To Success in

Life & Business: A Virgin Entrepreneur

Steve Jobs - Top 13 Secrets To Success in Life &

Business: The Power Of Think Different

www.ingramcontent.com/pod-product-compliance
Lightning Source LLC
Chambersburg PA
CBHW060153290526
45789CB00003B/1024